# Unlocking AI in Digital Marketing: Strategies for Success in the AI Era

By Simon Foote © 2024

# Contents

## Introduction

- What is AI and how is it relevant to digital marketing?

- Brief overview of AI applications in marketing

- Benefits and challenges of using AI in marketing

## Chapter 1: AI and Marketing Automation

- Email marketing automation with AI

- AI-powered chatbots and conversational marketing

- AI for lead scoring and nurturing

- Personalized product recommendations using AI

## Chapter 2: AI for Content Creation and Optimization

- AI content creation tools (writing, images, videos)

- Using AI for content ideation and topic modeling

- AI for content optimization (SEO, personalization)

- Multivariate content testing with AI

## Chapter 3: AI and Social Media Marketing

- Social listening and sentiment analysis with AI

- AI for social media content creation and curation

- Influencer marketing with AI audience analysis

- AI prediction of viral social media content

## Chapter 4: AI for Paid Advertising

- AI bid optimization and budget allocation

- AI creative generation for ad variations

- Using AI for targeted ad audience selection

- Landing page optimization with AI

## Chapter 5: AI for Marketing Analytics and Insights

- AI for analyzing large marketing datasets

- Predictive analytics using AI models

- Identifying market trends and customer insights with AI

- Optimizing marketing mix with AI attribution modeling

# Chapter 6: AI and Customer Experience

- AI chatbots and virtual assistants for customer service

- Personalized user experiences powered by AI

- AI recommendation engines for ecommerce

- Predictive customer behavior modeling with AI

# Chapter 7: Practical AI Implementation

- Evaluating AI marketing tools and services

- Data requirements and preparation for AI marketing

- Integrating AI with existing marketing technology stack

- AI talent - training teams or outsourcing needs

## Chapter 8: Ethical Considerations with AI Marketing

- Bias and transparency concerns with AI algorithms

- Privacy issues with AI data collection

- Brand trust and disclosure around AI usage

- Accountability frameworks for AI decision-making

# Conclusion

- Looking ahead - future of AI in marketing

- AI marketing strategies for competitive advantage

- Limitations of current AI capabilities

# Introduction

Welcome to "Unlocking AI in Digital Marketing: Strategies for Success in the AI Era." In this book, we embark on a journey to explore the intersection of artificial intelligence (AI) and digital marketing, uncovering the transformative power of AI technologies in shaping the future of marketing.

The digital landscape is evolving at an

unprecedented pace, driven by advancements in AI and machine learning. From automating routine tasks to delivering personalized customer experiences, AI has revolutionized how businesses engage with their audience, optimize campaigns, and drive growth.

In today's hyper-connected world, consumers expect more than ever before from brands. They crave personalized experiences, relevant content, and seamless interactions across channels. This demand for hyper-personalization and real-time engagement presents both opportunities and challenges for marketers.

This book serves as your guide to navigating the complex terrain of AI-powered digital marketing. Whether you're a seasoned marketer looking to stay ahead of the curve or a newcomer eager to harness the potential of AI, you'll find practical insights, strategies, and best practices to propel your marketing efforts to new heights.

Throughout the chapters that follow, we'll delve into the myriad ways AI is reshaping every aspect of the marketing funnel, from lead generation and customer acquisition to retention and advocacy.

We'll explore cutting-edge AI applications in email marketing, content creation, social media, paid advertising, analytics, customer experience, and more.

But it's not just about the technology. As we journey through the world of AI in marketing, we'll also confront the ethical considerations and challenges that accompany its adoption. From concerns about data privacy and algorithmic bias to transparency and accountability, we'll examine how marketers can navigate the ethical landscape of AI with integrity and responsibility.

Above all, this book is a call to action—a call to embrace the opportunities that AI presents, to innovate fearlessly, and to redefine what's possible in the realm of digital marketing.

Whether you're a marketer, business leader, or technology enthusiast, "Unlocking AI in Digital Marketing" invites you to join us on this transformative journey as we unlock the full potential of AI to shape the future of marketing.

# Chapter 1: AI and Marketing Automation

The marketing technology landscape has exploded with an abundance of automation tools that aim to streamline processes, drive efficiencies, and improve overall productivity. At the core of many modern marketing automation platforms is artificial intelligence (AI) working behind the scenes to power intelligent workflows, predictions, and decision-making capabilities.

## Email Marketing Automation with AI

Email remains one of the most effective marketing channels with a massive return on investment potential. However, successfully executing an email marketing strategy requires carefully segmented contact lists, perfectly timed campaigns, highly personalized content, and continual optimization based on results.

This is where AI can be a game-changer for email marketers. AI algorithms can analyze huge volumes of user data - website behavior, purchase histories, email engagement patterns and more - to predict the optimal time to send emails and automate the delivery for maximum open rates.

AI natural language processing (NLP) models can

automatically generate the most relevant email copy and subject lines based on the contact's profile and interests. And machine learning prediction models continually optimize content and delivery cadences by identifying patterns that lead to higher conversions.

Leading email marketing services like HubSpot, Marketo, ActiveCampaign and others now provide AI-powered features such as smart content, send-time optimization and predictive analytics to supercharge marketing automation workflows.

## AI-Powered Chatbots and Conversational Marketing

With users increasingly demanding instant gratification, chatbots have gone mainstream as a way to provide 24/7 automated conversational support. AI virtual assistants can handle common customer queries, qualify sales leads, provide product information and recommendations, or assist with routine transactions.

More advanced AI chatbots can engage in dynamic back-and-forth conversations using NLP to understand context and intent from free-form user inputs. This allows for highly personalized interactions akin to conversing with a human agent.

Chatbots can be deployed on company websites, mobile apps, messaging platforms like Facebook Messenger,

WhatsApp and more. AI chatbots provide an always-available touchpoint to capture leads, nurture prospects through the funnel, or provide customer service - improving marketing efficiencies and customer experiences.

## AI for Lead Scoring and Nurturing

One of the biggest challenges in B2B marketing is identifying the "hot" leads from large pools of prospects at different stages of the buying journey.

Manually prioritizing and nurturing each lead is extremely time-consuming and inefficient.

AI and machine learning models can automatically analyze lead data - firmographic information, content engagement, interactions with sales teams and more - to score and prioritize the hottest leads for immediate sales pursuit. Lower-scoring leads are automatically nurtured through AI-driven campaigns until their engagement signals that they are sales-ready.

Tools like Marketo, Pardot and Eloqua use AI lead scoring to predict the hottest leads and automate the routing to sales while lower-priority leads receive personalized content streams, offer updates and automated check-ins to progress them through the nurture cycle. Marketing automation is streamlined while boosting conversions.

# Personalized Product Recommendations Using AI

On the e-commerce side, AI recommendation engines work behind the scenes to provide consumers with hyper-personalized product recommendations tailored to their interests and purchase histories.

Companies like Amazon, Netflix, Spotify and others use AI to analyze troves of user data - browsing activity, purchases, ratings, consumption patterns and more - to surface recommendations that will most likely result in conversions or engagement for that specific customer.

Machine learning models find unexpected correlations and similarities between product attributes, user profiles and behaviors patterns to make accurate predictive recommendations in real-time as users navigate digital touchpoints.

AI not only provides better personalized user experiences but drives higher average order values and customer lifetime value by recommending complementary products, upgrades and effectively cross or upselling.

As marketing automation and personalization capabilities continue advancing with AI, brands will be able to gain a significant competitive advantage by more efficiently attracting, nurturing and converting more prospects into loyal, lucrative customers.

# Chapter 2: AI for Content Creation and Optimization

Content marketing has become an integral part of any successful digital marketing strategy. Creating high-quality, educational or entertaining content helps brands build trust, generate leads, and drive sales. However, producing a steady stream of fresh, relevant content is challenging and resource-intensive.

This is where AI can be a powerful tool for streamlining

content workflows while improving quality, relevance and performance. AI is impacting all stages of the content lifecycle - from ideation and creation to optimization and delivery.

## AI Content Creation Tools

Perhaps the most direct application of AI in content marketing is using AI writing tools to actually generate marketing copy, blogs, articles, scripts, product descriptions and more. While these AI writers are not intended to fully replace human copywriters, they can draft drafts, expand outlines, or provide a starting point that human editors can polish.

Tools like CopyAI, Jasper and Writesonic leverage large language models trained on massive text datasets to understand context and generate fluent, natural-sounding content on virtually any topic. These AI writers excel at tasks like ideation, research consolidation, and rewriting existing content in different tones or formats.

For visual content, AI tools like DALL-E, Midjourney and Stable Diffusion use text-to-image generation to create custom images and graphics based on written prompts. This AI-powered graphic design can produce customized visuals for blogs, social media posts and marketing campaigns on-demand, drastically cutting costs and timelines.

There are also AI tools for generating videos, 3D animations, voiceovers, music and more, expanding AI's applications for streamlining multimedia content creation processes.

Using AI for Content Ideation and Topic Modeling

Even before any content creation occurs, AI can analyze search data, web trends and competitor content to surface topics with high interest and engagement potential. AI topic modeling uncovers semantically related keywords and entities that human strategists may miss.

Search data can reveal content gaps that need to be filled. Social media listening tools infused with AI can identify conversations and questions users are engaging with around a brand or product category.

AI-powered insights can fuel content calendars and strategies aligned with actual audience needs, not just gut instincts. Tools like BrightEdge, Clearscope, and MarketMuse use AI to guide content planning, optimize production workflows, and benchmark performance.

AI for Content Optimization

Once content is created, AI can optimize it to outperform competitors and meet search engine requirements. Google's AI-powered rankbrain algorithm understands query contexts, entities and content relevance.

AI content optimization tools can analyze content drafts and ensure proper topical keyword coverage, answer relevant questions with detailed information, hit optimal word counts, check reading levels, fix grammar issues and more.

For example, AI tools from companies like Surfer SEO and Clearscope crawl the top-ranking content for target keywords and provide real-time customized briefs for creating superior content assets.

AI also enables real-time content adaptation and micro-personalization at the moment of engagement. AI models can dynamically modify website content, emails or ads based on the specific visitor's interests, location, device or behavioral data for maximum relevance and impact.

Multivariate Content Testing with AI

Testing different content variations to determine top performers is critical, but managing that process is time and labor-intensive. AI and machine learning enable automated multivariate testing at massive scale.

Cloud-based content management platforms like Evergage, Instapage and Optimizely use AI models to rapidly generate multiple content versions with variable headlines, images, text blocks,

CTAs and more. As visitor traffic flows in, built-in AI monitors engagement metrics and continuously optimizes to double down on high-performing variants.

These tools essentially automate the A/B testing process with little human intervention, while using machine learning to exploit winning content combinations faster than manual processes. AI-powered testing accelerates finding the most impactful content for improving metrics like click-through rates, conversions, engagement and ROI.

With a constellation of AI capabilities like automated creation, optimization and testing of marketing content assets, content teams can amplify their production volume, quality and impact to engage audiences and drive business results. AI is modernizing content marketing processes and efficacy.

# Chapter 3: AI and Social Media Marketing

## Social Listening and Sentiment Analysis with AI

In today's digital landscape, social media has become a powerful platform for businesses to connect with their audience, gather insights, and monitor public sentiment towards their brand. AI plays a crucial role in social listening and sentiment analysis, enabling companies to process vast amounts of data from various social media channels efficiently.

AI-powered social listening tools can scour through millions of posts, comments, and mentions across platforms like Twitter, Facebook, Instagram, and Reddit. These tools employ natural language processing (NLP) and machine learning algorithms to analyze the content and identify relevant conversations, topics, and trends related to a brand, product, or industry.

Sentiment analysis is a critical aspect of social listening, as it helps businesses understand the emotional tone and sentiment behind social media conversations. AI algorithms can analyze the language used in posts, comments, and reviews to determine whether the sentiment is positive, negative, or neutral. This insight is invaluable for brands to gauge public opinion, identify potential issues, and respond promptly to customer concerns or complaints.

Furthermore, AI-powered sentiment analysis can go beyond surface-level sentiment classification by detecting sarcasm, irony, and subtle nuances in language. This advanced analysis enables businesses to gain a more accurate understanding of consumer sentiment and tailor their social media strategies accordingly.

## AI for Social Media Content Creation and Curation

In the fast-paced world of social media, creating engaging and relevant content is paramount for businesses to capture their audience's attention and maintain a strong online presence. AI offers a range of solutions to streamline content creation and curation processes.

AI-powered content creation tools can assist in generating social media posts, captions, and ad copy. These tools leverage natural language generation (NLG) algorithms to produce human-like text based on provided inputs, such as keywords, topics, or desired tone and style. This can significantly reduce the time and effort required for content creation, freeing up marketers to focus on strategy and creative direction.

AI can also aid in content curation by analyzing vast amounts of data from various sources, including social media platforms, news websites, and industry publications. Machine learning algorithms can identify relevant and trending topics, articles, or posts that align with a brand's content strategy. This curated content can then be shared on social media channels, increasing engagement and establishing thought leadership.

Additionally, AI can optimize the timing and frequency of social media posts by analyzing historical data and user behavior patterns. This ensures that content is delivered at optimal times, maximizing reach and engagement.

# Influencer Marketing with AI Audience Analysis

Influencer marketing has emerged as a powerful strategy for brands to reach and engage with their target audiences on social media. AI plays a crucial role in identifying and analyzing influencers and their audiences, enabling more effective influencer marketing campaigns.

AI-powered tools can analyze vast amounts of social media data to identify influential individuals or accounts within a specific niche or industry.

These tools consider various factors, such as follower count, engagement rates, content relevance, and audience demographics, to determine the most suitable influencers for a brand's campaign.

Furthermore, AI can provide in-depth audience analysis for influencers, providing valuable insights into their followers' interests, behaviors, and demographics. This information aids brands in selecting influencers whose audiences align closely with their target market, increasing the likelihood of successful campaign outcomes.

AI can also assist in monitoring and evaluating the performance of influencer marketing campaigns. Machine learning algorithms can track engagement metrics, sentiment analysis, and campaign reach, providing data-driven insights for optimizing future campaigns and maximizing return on investment (ROI).

AI Prediction of Viral Social Media Content

One of the holy grails of social media marketing is the ability to predict which content will go viral. While predicting virality with absolute certainty remains a challenge, AI offers valuable tools and techniques to improve the chances of creating viral content.

AI algorithms can analyze vast amounts of historical social media data, including posts, engagement metrics, and user behavior patterns, to identify common characteristics and patterns of viral content. These insights can inform content creation strategies, helping brands craft content that resonates with their target audience and has a higher likelihood of being shared widely.

Machine learning models can also be trained to predict the virality potential of new content by analyzing various features, such as language, images, videos, and accompanying metadata. These models can provide scores or probabilities indicating the potential for a piece of content to go viral, enabling brands to refine and optimize their content before publishing.

Predictive analytics powered by AI can also help brands identify emerging trends and topics that are gaining traction on social media. By incorporating these insights into their content strategies, brands can stay ahead of the curve and capitalize on viral opportunities as they arise.

While AI cannot guarantee viral success, its predictive capabilities can significantly enhance the chances of creating shareable, engaging content that resonates with audiences and drives social media marketing goals.

# Chapter 4: AI for Paid Advertising

Paid advertising is a crucial component of digital marketing strategies, and AI has revolutionized how advertisers optimize their campaigns for maximum impact and efficiency. In this chapter, we'll delve into the various ways AI is transforming paid advertising, from bid optimization to creative generation and audience targeting.

## AI Bid Optimization and Budget Allocation

Traditionally, advertisers relied on manual bid adjustments and budget allocations based on historical data and intuition. However, AI-driven bid optimization algorithms now enable marketers to dynamically adjust bids in real-time based on a multitude of factors such as user behavior, device, location, time of day, and even weather conditions.

These AI algorithms leverage machine learning models to analyze vast amounts of data and predict the likelihood of conversion for each ad impression. By continuously optimizing bids, advertisers can maximize their return on investment (ROI) and achieve their desired advertising goals, whether it's maximizing conversions, increasing website traffic, or improving brand awareness.

Moreover, AI-powered budget allocation algorithms help marketers distribute their advertising budgets more effectively across different campaigns, channels, and audience segments. By automatically reallocating budgets to high-performing campaigns and scaling back on underperforming ones, advertisers can optimize their overall advertising spend and achieve better results within their budget constraints.

## AI Creative Generation for Ad Variations

Creating compelling ad creatives that resonate with the target audience is essential for the success of any advertising campaign. AI has introduced innovative solutions to streamline the creative process and generate personalized ad variations at scale.

AI-driven creative generation platforms leverage techniques such as natural language processing (NLP) and computer vision to automatically generate ad copy, headlines, images, and even videos tailored to specific audience segments. These platforms analyze historical performance data, audience demographics, and contextual information to generate highly relevant and engaging ad content.

Furthermore, AI-powered creative optimization algorithms continuously test and iterate ad variations to identify the most effective combinations of elements that drive the desired outcomes. By automating the creative optimization process, advertisers can save time and resources while maximizing the performance of their advertising campaigns.

## Using AI for Targeted Ad Audience Selection

One of the key advantages of digital advertising is the ability to target ads to specific audience segments based on their demographics, interests, behavior, and other criteria. AI-powered audience targeting algorithms enhance this capability by analyzing vast amounts of data to identify high-value audience segments and optimize ad targeting strategies.

These algorithms utilize machine learning techniques to analyze user data from various sources, such as website visits, app usage, social media interactions, and third-party data providers. By identifying patterns and correlations in user behavior, AI algorithms can accurately predict which audience segments are most likely to respond positively to specific ad messages and offers.

Moreover, AI-driven audience segmentation algorithms enable advertisers to create highly granular audience segments based on nuanced characteristics and behaviors. This level of granularity allows marketers to tailor their ad creative and messaging to resonate with each segment's unique preferences and needs, resulting in higher engagement and conversion rates.

## Landing Page Optimization with AI

The effectiveness of a paid advertising campaign doesn't end with the ad itself; the landing page experience plays a crucial role in converting ad clicks into meaningful actions, such as purchases, sign-ups, or inquiries. AI-powered landing page optimization tools help marketers improve the performance of their landing pages and enhance the overall user experience.

These tools utilize machine learning algorithms to analyze user behavior on landing pages, such as bounce rates, time on page, scroll depth, and conversion rates. By identifying patterns and trends in user interaction data, AI algorithms can identify areas for improvement and recommend optimizations to increase conversion rates.

Furthermore, AI-driven A/B testing platforms enable marketers to test multiple variations of landing pages simultaneously and automatically identify the winning variation based on predefined success metrics. This iterative testing approach allows advertisers to continuously refine their landing page designs and messaging to maximize conversion rates and ROI.

In conclusion, AI is revolutionizing paid advertising by enabling advertisers to optimize bids, generate personalized ad creatives, target specific audience segments, and enhance landing page experiences. By leveraging AI-powered tools and algorithms, marketers can achieve better results, improve efficiency, and stay ahead in today's competitive digital advertising landscape.

# Chapter 5: AI for Marketing Analytics and Insights

Marketing analytics is the backbone of data-driven decision-making in modern businesses. With the proliferation of data sources and the increasing complexity of consumer behavior, marketers are turning to AI to extract actionable insights and drive strategic initiatives. In this comprehensive chapter, we will explore the diverse applications of AI in marketing analytics, from analyzing large datasets to predicting future trends and optimizing marketing strategies.

### AI for Analyzing Large Marketing Datasets

The volume and variety of marketing data generated across multiple channels, including websites, social media, email campaigns, and customer interactions, can be overwhelming for marketers to analyze manually. AI-powered analytics platforms offer scalable solutions to process and analyze large datasets efficiently.

Machine learning algorithms, such as clustering, classification, and regression, enable marketers to uncover patterns, trends, and correlations in their data that may not be apparent through traditional analysis methods. By automatically identifying insights and anomalies, AI algorithms empower marketers to make data-driven decisions and optimize their marketing strategies for better outcomes.

Furthermore, AI-driven data visualization tools provide intuitive interfaces for exploring and interpreting complex marketing data. Interactive dashboards, heatmaps, and predictive models enable marketers to gain actionable insights at a glance and communicate findings effectively to stakeholders across the organization.

### Predictive Analytics Using AI Models

Predictive analytics leverages historical data to forecast future trends, behaviors, and outcomes. AI-powered predictive models enhance the accuracy and granularity of these forecasts by incorporating advanced machine learning techniques and analyzing vast amounts of data.

For example, predictive lead scoring models use AI algorithms to analyze past customer interactions, demographic data, and behavioral patterns to identify leads with the highest likelihood of conversion. By prioritizing leads based on their propensity to purchase, marketers can focus their resources on prospects with the greatest potential value and improve sales effectiveness.

Similarly, churn prediction models use AI to analyze customer data and predict which customers are at risk of churning or canceling their subscriptions. By proactively targeting at-risk customers with personalized retention offers or interventions, marketers can reduce churn rates and increase customer lifetime value.

### Identifying Market Trends and Customer Insights with AI

Understanding market trends and consumer preferences is essential for developing successful marketing strategies and staying ahead of the competition. AI-powered trend analysis tools analyze large volumes of unstructured data from social media, news articles, and other sources to identify emerging trends and topics of interest.

Natural language processing (NLP) algorithms enable marketers to analyze text data and extract insights from customer reviews, survey responses, and social media conversations. Sentiment analysis algorithms categorize opinions and emotions expressed in text data, allowing marketers to gauge customer sentiment and identify areas for improvement.

Moreover, AI-driven market segmentation algorithms enable marketers to divide their target audience into homogeneous groups based on demographic, behavioral, and psychographic characteristics. By understanding the unique needs and preferences of different segments, marketers can tailor their messaging, offers, and product experiences to resonate with each audience segment effectively.

### Optimizing Marketing Mix with AI Attribution Modeling

Attribution modeling is the process of determining the relative contribution of each marketing touchpoint to a desired outcome, such as a conversion or sale. AI-powered attribution models analyze customer journey data across multiple channels and devices to attribute credit accurately to each marketing interaction.

Traditional attribution models, such as first-click, last-click, or linear attribution, often oversimplify the complexity of modern consumer journeys and fail to account for the interplay between different marketing channels. AI-driven attribution models, such as algorithmic attribution or machine learning-based models, dynamically adjust credit allocation based on the unique characteristics of each conversion path.

By accurately attributing value to each touchpoint along the customer journey, marketers can optimize their marketing mix, allocate budgets more effectively, and maximize the impact of their marketing investments. Moreover, AI-powered attribution models provide insights into the interdependencies between different channels and help marketers identify synergies and optimization opportunities.

In conclusion, AI is transforming marketing

analytics by enabling marketers to analyze large datasets, predict future trends, uncover customer insights, and optimize marketing strategies with unprecedented accuracy and efficiency. By harnessing the power of AI-driven analytics tools and algorithms, marketers can gain a competitive edge and drive sustainable growth in today's data-driven business landscape.

# Chapter 6: AI and Customer Experience

In the digital age, customer experience (CX) has emerged as a critical competitive differentiator for businesses across industries. AI technologies are revolutionizing the way brands interact with customers, delivering personalized and seamless experiences at scale. This chapter explores the multifaceted role of AI in enhancing customer experience, from AI-powered chatbots to predictive customer behavior modeling.

### AI Chatbots and Virtual Assistants for Customer Service

AI-powered chatbots and virtual assistants have become ubiquitous in modern customer service operations, enabling businesses to provide instant support and assistance to customers 24/7. These AI systems leverage natural language processing (NLP) and machine learning algorithms to understand and respond to customer inquiries in real-time.

Chatbots can handle a wide range of customer interactions, including answering frequently asked questions, assisting with product recommendations, troubleshooting issues, and processing orders or reservations. By automating routine tasks and inquiries, chatbots free up human agents to focus on more complex and high-value interactions, improving overall efficiency and customer satisfaction.

Furthermore, AI-driven chatbots continuously learn from interactions with customers, allowing them to improve over time and deliver more accurate and personalized responses. As a result, businesses can provide consistent and frictionless customer experiences across various channels, including websites, mobile apps, social media platforms, and messaging apps.

### Personalized User Experiences Powered by AI

Personalization has become a cornerstone of effective customer experience strategies, as customers increasingly expect tailored interactions and recommendations from brands. AI technologies enable businesses to deliver highly personalized user experiences by analyzing vast amounts of customer data and predicting individual preferences and behaviors.

For example, AI-powered recommendation engines analyze customer purchase history, browsing behavior, and demographic information to suggest products or content that are relevant to each user's interests and preferences. By presenting personalized recommendations at the right time and through the right channels, businesses can increase customer engagement, conversion rates, and customer lifetime value.

Moreover, AI-driven personalization extends beyond product recommendations to encompass personalized marketing messages, offers, and promotions. By segmenting customers based on their unique characteristics and behaviors, businesses can deliver targeted communications that resonate with each audience segment, driving higher response rates and customer loyalty.

### AI Recommendation Engines for E-commerce

E-commerce platforms rely heavily on recommendation engines to drive product discovery and increase average order value. AI-powered recommendation engines analyze vast amounts of transactional and behavioral data to identify patterns and correlations between products and customer preferences.

These recommendation engines employ collaborative filtering, content-based filtering, and hybrid recommendation algorithms to generate personalized product recommendations for individual users. By understanding each customer's browsing history, purchase behavior, and preferences, recommendation engines can suggest relevant products that are likely to resonate with their interests.

Furthermore, AI-driven recommendation engines can enhance cross-selling and upselling opportunities by recommending complementary or higher-priced products to customers based on their purchase history and browsing behavior. By surfacing relevant recommendations during the shopping journey, businesses can increase customer satisfaction and drive incremental revenue.

### Predictive Customer Behavior Modeling with AI

Predictive analytics techniques enable businesses to anticipate future customer behaviors and preferences, allowing them to proactively address customer needs and deliver personalized experiences. AI-powered predictive models analyze historical data and external factors to forecast customer behaviors, such as purchase intent, churn propensity, and lifetime value.

For example, churn prediction models use machine learning algorithms to analyze customer engagement metrics, usage patterns, and demographic information to identify customers who are at risk of churning. By intervening with targeted retention strategies, such as personalized offers or proactive support, businesses can reduce churn rates and increase customer retention.

Similarly, predictive lead scoring models help businesses prioritize and qualify leads based on their likelihood to convert into paying customers. By analyzing lead characteristics, behavior, and engagement signals, AI algorithms can identify high-quality leads that are most likely to generate revenue, enabling sales teams to focus their efforts on the most promising opportunities.

In conclusion, AI is revolutionizing customer experience by enabling businesses to deliver personalized and seamless interactions across various touchpoints. From AI chatbots and recommendation engines to predictive customer behavior modeling, AI technologies empower businesses to anticipate customer needs, drive engagement, and build long-lasting relationships with their customers. By embracing AI-driven customer experience strategies, businesses can gain a competitive edge and differentiate themselves in today's crowded marketplace.

# Chapter 7: Practical AI Implementation

Implementing AI in marketing requires careful planning, strategic alignment, and the right combination of technology, talent, and resources. In this chapter, we'll explore the practical aspects of AI implementation, from evaluating AI marketing tools to integrating AI into existing marketing technology stacks.

### Evaluating AI Marketing Tools and Services

The AI landscape is vast and diverse, with a multitude of tools and services available to marketers across various domains, including analytics, automation, content creation, and customer experience. When evaluating AI marketing tools and services, it's essential to consider several factors:

- **Functionality**: Assess whether the tool or service addresses specific marketing needs and objectives, such as improving lead generation, enhancing customer segmentation, or optimizing advertising campaigns.

- **Accuracy and Performance**: Evaluate the accuracy and performance of AI algorithms and models, as well as their ability to deliver actionable insights and measurable results.

- **Ease of Use**: Consider the usability and user interface of the tool or service, as well as the level of technical expertise required for implementation and usage.

- **Integration Capabilities**: Determine whether the tool or service integrates seamlessly with existing marketing systems, such as CRM platforms, email marketing software, or analytics tools.

- **Cost and ROI**: Evaluate the cost-effectiveness of the tool or service in relation to the expected return on investment (ROI) and the value it provides to the organization.

By conducting thorough evaluations and pilot tests, marketers can identify the most suitable AI marketing tools and services that align with their business goals and requirements.

### Data Requirements and Preparation for AI Marketing

Data is the fuel that powers AI algorithms and models, making data quality, accessibility, and relevance crucial considerations for successful AI implementation in marketing. Marketers must ensure that they have access to clean, comprehensive, and relevant data to train AI models effectively.

Data preparation involves several key steps:

- **Data Collection**: Gather data from various sources, including customer interactions, transactional records, website analytics, and social media platforms.

- **Data Cleaning**: Cleanse and preprocess the data to remove duplicates, errors, and inconsistencies, ensuring that the data is accurate and reliable for analysis.

- **Data Integration**: Integrate data from disparate sources into a unified data repository or data warehouse, enabling holistic analysis and insights generation.

- **Feature Engineering**: Extract and transform relevant features from the raw data to feed into AI models, enhancing their predictive power and performance.

- **Data Governance and Compliance**: Ensure compliance with data privacy regulations, such as GDPR or CCPA, and implement robust data governance practices to protect customer privacy and security.

By investing in robust data management practices and infrastructure, marketers can unlock the full potential of AI and derive actionable insights that drive business growth and innovation.

### Integrating AI with Existing Marketing Technology Stack

Successful AI implementation requires seamless integration with existing marketing technology stacks and workflows. Marketers should carefully assess how AI solutions fit within their current infrastructure and processes and identify integration points and dependencies.

Key considerations for integrating AI with existing marketing technology stack include:

- **API and SDK Compatibility**: Ensure that AI solutions offer APIs or software development kits (SDKs) that enable integration with popular marketing platforms and systems.

- **Data Exchange and Synchronization**: Establish data pipelines and integration mechanisms to exchange data between AI systems and other marketing systems, such as CRM, email marketing, or advertising platforms.

- **Workflow Automation**: Automate repetitive tasks and processes using AI-driven workflow automation tools, streamlining marketing operations and improving efficiency.

- **Training and Onboarding**: Provide training and support to marketing teams to familiarize them with AI tools and technologies and enable them to leverage AI capabilities effectively.

- **Performance Monitoring and Optimization**: Implement monitoring and reporting mechanisms to track the performance and impact of AI implementations on key marketing metrics and KPIs, enabling continuous improvement and optimization.

By integrating AI seamlessly into their existing marketing technology stack, marketers can leverage AI capabilities to enhance their workflows, drive innovation, and achieve better outcomes across the marketing lifecycle.

### AI Talent - Training Teams or Outsourcing Needs

Building and nurturing AI talent is essential for successful AI implementation in marketing. Marketers have the option to either train existing teams in AI skills or outsource AI capabilities to external vendors or agencies.

Training internal teams involves:

- **Skills Development**: Provide training and upskilling programs to equip marketing teams with AI-related skills and knowledge, such as data analysis, machine learning, and programming.

- **Cross-functional Collaboration**: Foster collaboration between marketing, data science, and IT teams to leverage diverse expertise and perspectives in AI implementation projects.

- **Experimentation and Innovation**: Encourage a culture of experimentation and innovation, where team members are empowered to explore new AI technologies and approaches to solve marketing challenges.

Alternatively, outsourcing AI capabilities to external vendors or agencies offers several advantages:

- **Access to Specialized Expertise**: Tap into the expertise and experience of AI specialists and data scientists who specialize in marketing applications and technologies.

- **Scalability and Flexibility**: Scale AI capabilities up or down according to evolving business needs and priorities, without the overhead of maintaining an in-house team.

- **Time and Cost Savings**: Reduce time-to-market and implementation costs by leveraging pre-built AI solutions and frameworks offered by external vendors.

Ultimately, the decision to train internal teams or outsource AI capabilities depends on factors such as organizational resources, strategic priorities, and the complexity of AI implementation projects.

By investing in talent development and strategic partnerships, marketers can build a solid foundation for AI implementation and drive sustainable growth and innovation in their marketing initiatives.

# Chapter 8: Ethical Considerations with AI Marketing

As artificial intelligence (AI) continues to permeate various aspects of marketing, it brings with it a host of ethical considerations and challenges. In this chapter, we delve into the ethical implications of AI in marketing, including issues related to bias, transparency, privacy, and accountability, and explore frameworks for ethical AI decision-making.

### Bias and Transparency Concerns with AI Algorithms

One of the most significant ethical concerns surrounding AI in marketing is the potential for bias in algorithms. AI algorithms learn from historical data, which may reflect societal biases or prejudices, leading to biased outcomes in decision-making processes such as targeting, personalization, and recommendation.

To mitigate bias in AI algorithms, marketers must:

- **Diverse Dataset Representation**: Ensure that training datasets are diverse, inclusive, and representative of the target audience to minimize bias in AI models.

- **Algorithmic Fairness**: Implement fairness-aware algorithms that explicitly account for fairness criteria, such as demographic parity or equalized odds, to prevent discriminatory outcomes.

- **Continuous Monitoring and Evaluation**: Regularly monitor AI systems for bias and discrimination using metrics and evaluation frameworks and take corrective actions as necessary to address any biases that arise.

Transparency is another crucial aspect of ethical AI in marketing. Marketers should strive to make AI-driven decision-making processes transparent and understandable to consumers, allowing them to make informed choices and understand the basis for algorithmic recommendations.

### Privacy Issues with AI Data Collection

AI-powered marketing relies heavily on data collection and analysis to deliver personalized experiences and targeted advertisements. However, the widespread collection and processing of personal data raise significant privacy concerns, particularly regarding consent, data security, and user control over their data.

To address privacy issues in AI marketing, marketers should:

- **Privacy by Design**: Incorporate privacy principles and best practices into the design and development of AI systems from the outset, prioritizing data minimization, purpose limitation, and user consent.

- **Data Encryption and Security**: Implement robust data encryption and security measures to protect sensitive consumer data from unauthorized access, breaches, and misuse.

- **Transparent Data Practices**: Clearly communicate to consumers how their data is collected, used, and shared, including the types of data collected, the purposes of data processing, and their rights regarding their data.

- **Granular Consent Mechanisms**: Provide users with granular consent options and controls over their data, allowing them to opt-in or opt-out of specific data collection and processing activities.

By prioritizing privacy and adopting transparent data practices, marketers can build trust with consumers and demonstrate their commitment to ethical data handling and privacy protection.

### Brand Trust and Disclosure around AI Usage

Maintaining trust and credibility is paramount for brands leveraging AI in marketing. Consumers expect transparency and honesty from brands regarding the use of AI technologies, including how AI is employed, the data it collects, and the implications for consumers.

To foster trust and transparency around AI usage, marketers should:

- **Clear Communication**: Clearly communicate to consumers how AI is used in marketing activities, including the benefits, limitations, and potential risks associated with AI-driven personalization and targeting.

- **Ethical Guidelines and Policies**: Establish internal ethical guidelines and policies governing the use of AI in marketing, including principles for responsible AI usage, data ethics, and consumer privacy protection.

- **Third-Party Audits and Certification**: Subject AI systems and algorithms to independent audits and certification processes to validate their adherence to ethical standards and regulatory requirements.

- **Consumer Education**: Educate consumers about AI technologies and their implications for marketing, empowering them to make informed decisions about their data and privacy.

Transparency and accountability are essential for building and maintaining consumer trust in AI-driven marketing practices.

### Accountability Frameworks for AI Decision-Making

As AI assumes greater decision-making authority in marketing, establishing accountability frameworks becomes imperative to ensure responsible and ethical AI usage. Marketers should implement mechanisms to hold AI systems and their operators accountable for their actions and outcomes.

Key components of accountability frameworks for AI decision-making include:

- **Responsibility Assignment**: Clearly define roles and responsibilities for AI development, deployment, and monitoring, assigning accountability to individuals or teams for AI-related decisions and actions.

- **Explainability and Auditability**: Ensure that AI algorithms and models are explainable and auditable, allowing stakeholders to understand how decisions are made and assess the fairness and ethical implications of AI-driven outcomes.

- **Error Correction and Redress Mechanisms**:

Establish procedures for addressing errors, biases, or unintended consequences arising from AI decision-making, including mechanisms for redress and compensation for affected individuals.

- **Regulatory Compliance**: Ensure compliance with relevant laws, regulations, and industry standards governing AI usage in marketing, including data protection, anti-discrimination, and consumer protection laws.

By implementing robust accountability frameworks, marketers can enhance transparency, mitigate risks, and promote responsible AI decision-making in marketing activities.

### Conclusion

Ethical considerations play a central role in the responsible adoption and use of AI in marketing. Marketers must prioritize fairness, transparency, privacy, and accountability in their AI-driven initiatives to build trust with consumers and uphold ethical standards. By adopting ethical AI practices and frameworks, marketers can harness the power of AI to drive innovation, enhance customer experiences, and create value while ensuring that AI benefits society as a whole.

# Conclusion

In conclusion, "Unlocking AI in Digital Marketing: Strategies for Success in the AI Era" delves into the transformative potential of artificial intelligence (AI) in revolutionizing various facets of the marketing landscape. Throughout the book, we've explored the diverse applications of AI across different marketing domains, from automation and content creation to social media marketing, paid advertising, analytics, customer experience, and beyond.

AI has emerged as a powerful tool for marketers to enhance efficiency, optimize campaigns, personalize experiences, and drive meaningful engagement with consumers. By leveraging AI technologies such as machine learning, natural language processing, and predictive analytics, marketers can unlock valuable insights from vast amounts of data, automate routine tasks, and deliver personalized and seamless experiences across multiple touchpoints.

However, as AI continues to reshape the marketing landscape, it also brings with it a host of ethical considerations and challenges that must be addressed responsibly. From concerns about bias and transparency in AI algorithms to privacy issues surrounding data collection and usage, marketers must navigate a complex ethical landscape to ensure that AI-driven initiatives uphold principles of fairness, transparency, privacy, and accountability.

Building trust with consumers is paramount in the AI-driven marketing era. Marketers must prioritize transparency, honesty, and ethical data practices to foster trust and credibility with consumers. By communicating openly about the use of AI, respecting user privacy, and implementing robust accountability frameworks, marketers can demonstrate their commitment to responsible AI usage and earn the trust of their audience.

Looking ahead, the future of AI in marketing holds immense promise for innovation and growth. As AI technologies continue to evolve and mature, marketers can expect to see further advancements in areas such as predictive analytics, conversational AI, and augmented intelligence, enabling them to unlock new opportunities for customer engagement and business success.

Ultimately, "Unlocking AI in Digital Marketing: Strategies for Success in the AI Era" serves as a comprehensive guide for marketers seeking to leverage AI effectively to drive results and navigate the ethical considerations inherent in AI-driven marketing initiatives. By embracing AI technologies responsibly and ethically, marketers can not only stay ahead of the curve in today's competitive landscape but also contribute to positive societal impact and sustainable growth in the digital age.

www.ingramcontent.com/pod-product-compliance
Lightning Source LLC
Chambersburg PA
CBHW071210240526
45470CB00018B/1694